Hispanic Heritage

Hispanic Heritage

Title List

Latinos Today

Facts and Figures

by Kenneth McIntosh

Mason Crest Publishers
Philadelphia

Mason Crest Publishers Inc.

370 Reed Road

Broomall, Pennsylvania 19008

(866) MCP-BOOK (toll free)

First printing

1 2 3 4 5 6 7 8 9 10

Library of Congress Cataloging-in-Publication Data

McIntosh, Kenneth, 1959 —

  Latinos today : facts and figures / by Ken McIntosh.

    p. cm. —— (Hispanic heritage)

  Includes bibliographical references and index.

  ISBN 1-59084-940-X   ISBN 1-59084-924-8 (series)

  1. Hispanic Americans—Miscellanea—Juvenile literature. 2. Hispanic Americans—Social conditions—Miscellanea—Juvenile literature. I. Title. II. Hispanic heritage (Philadelphia, Pa.)

  E184.S75M424 2005

  973'.0468—dc22

                              200402286

Interior design by Dianne Hodack and MK Bassett-Harvey.

Produced by Harding House Publishing Service, Inc., Vestal, NY.

Cover design by Dianne Hodack.

Printed and bound in the Hashemite Kingdom of Jordan.

Contents

Of all children under 18, **Latino** are **61%** in San Antonio, % in Los Angeles, **39%** in Miami d San Diego, and **36%** in Houston

Introduction

by José E. Limón, Ph.D.

ven before there was a United States, Hispanics were present in what would become this country. Beginning in the sixteenth century, Spanish explorers traversed North America, and their explorations encouraged settlement as early as the sixteenth century in what is now northern New Mexico and Florida, and as late as the mid-eighteenth century in what is now southern Texas and California.

Later, in the nineteenth century, following Spain's gradual withdrawal from the New World, Mexico in particular established its own distinctive presence in what is now the southwestern part of the United States, a presence reinforced in the first half of the twentieth century by substantial immigration from that country. At the close of the nineteenth century, the U.S. war with Spain brought Cuba and Puerto Rico into an interactive relationship with the United States, the latter in a special political and economic affiliation with the United States even as American power influenced the course of almost every other Latin American country.

The books in this series remind us of these historical origins, even as each explores the present reality of different Hispanic groups. Some of these books explore the contemporary social origins—what social scientists call the "push" factors—behind the accelerating Hispanic immigration to America: political instability, economic underdevelopment and crisis, environmental degradation, impoverished or wholly absent educational systems, and other circumstances contribute to many Latin Americans deciding they will be better off in the United States.

And, for the most part, they will be. The vast majority come to work and work very hard, in order to earn better wages than they would back home. They fill significant labor needs in the U.S. economy and contribute to the economy through lower consumer prices and sales taxes.

When they leave their home countries, many immigrants may initially fear that they are leaving behind vital and important aspects of their home cultures: the Spanish language, kinship ties, food, music, folklore, and the arts. But as these books also make clear, culture is a fluid thing, and these native cultures are not only brought to America, they are also replenished in the United States in fascinating and novel ways. These books further suggest to us that Hispanic groups enhance American culture as a whole.

Our country—especially the young, future leaders who will read these books—can only benefit by the fair and full knowledge these authors provide about the socio-historical origins and contemporary cultural manifestations of America's Hispanic heritage.

1

Latinos in the United States: Reaching for the Sky

At 1:30 in the morning of April 8, 1993, the night sky above Kennedy Space Station turned white, as if illuminated by a vast, flickering flashbulb. The Earth shook as the space shuttle *Discovery*, perched atop 4.5 million tons of booster and fuel, began its thunderous ascent into space. Among the five crew members aboard was Ellen Ochoa, Ph.D., the first Latina to journey beyond Earth's atmosphere.

Ellen Ochoa was the first Latina astronaut.

Selected by NASA in January 1990, Dr. Ochoa became an astronaut in July 1991. A veteran of four space flights, by 2004, she had logged over 978 hours outside Earth's gravity. She holds *patents* for a number of scientific discoveries and has done important work in the research and development of computer systems for space missions.

Reflecting on her life, Dr. Ochoa says, "I can only imagine the amazement and pride my grandparents would feel, having been born in Mexico in the 1870s, on knowing that their granddaughter grew up to travel in space. Their move to the United States to raise their family, along with my mother's passion for learning, provided me with the opportunity and motivation to get an education and set high goals."

Over the past five centuries, the descendants of Spanish colonists and New World natives have crossed barriers—of race, language, culture, discrimination, and geography—to achieve their dreams. Today, more than 40 million Latinos living in the United States profoundly shape this country. Many of them have suffered to gain respect, homes, education, and careers. They have learned well how to fight against the odds in pursuit of their dreams.

A Diverse Group

he first thing you need to know about Latinos is this—for everything you assume about this incredibly diverse group, there are just as many exceptions. Many Latinos speak Spanish—most are *bilingual*—but millions speak only English. Some are recent immigrants to the United States, but there are also millions whose ancestors were in this land before any English-speaking colonists arrived. Some have dark skin and black hair, the stereotyped "exotic Latin" look, but others are naturally blond and blue-eyed, while others are of African descent. Many are Catholic, but almost as many attend Pentecostal churches, and some worship as Buddhists or Muslims. Many enjoy *salsa* music or urban rap, yet others are accomplished classical musicians. Among 40 million people, there is understandably a vast amount of variety.

Even the terms "Latino" or "Hispanic" are debatable. D. H. Figueredo, who teaches college courses in Latino literature, explains the history of terms. "In the first half of the twentieth century, the label 'Spanish' was used to describe people . . . of Spanish descent." In the 1950s, the U.S. Census Bureau

patents: exclusive rights to market inventions.

bilingual: the ability to communicate in two languages.

salsa: a dance and music style that combines jazz and rock with African Cuban melodies.

11

A young Latina woman

invented the term "Spanish surname." At the same time, the media often used the word "Latin," because it conveyed a romantic notion of the "tall, dark, and handsome" Hollywood "Latin lover."

In the 1960s, the U.S. Census Bureau arrived at the briefer expression "Hispanic." The *New York Times* and other newspapers then popularized the term. Figueredo writes, " 'It is a term created by English speakers for an English-speaking audience, and today . . . Hispanics who accept the term do so because the word hints of middle class values."

The term "Hispanic" is favored by the majority of people from Cuban and Puerto Rican descent residing in Florida, and is acceptable to most Hispanics on the East Coast of the United States. In Texas, Arizona, and other parts of the Southwest, the term Hispanic is also accepted. A 2000 presidential tracking poll by Hispanic Trends Inc., a national *polling* firm, asked registered voters which term they preferred: Hispanic or Latino. The majority preferred the term Hispanic.

In the Midwest, however, the term Latino is favored. Further west, California Latinos tend to be passionate in their opposition to the word "Hispanic." Some outspoken Latinos and Latinas in other states also object to the term. Best-selling author and poet Sandra Cisneros identifies herself as Latina, Chicana, Tejana, and Mexican American, but never Hispanic. Cisneros is so offended by the term that she has refused to be pictured on the cover of *Hispanic* magazine. "The term Hispanic makes my skin crawl," Cisneros says. "It's a very *colonistic* term, a disrespectful term, a term imposed on us without asking what we wanted to call ourselves."

Figueredo describes the origins of the word "Latino": "Latino is a Spanish word. It has a gender: Latino for male, Latina for female. It is short for Latinoamericano, thus it looks more toward Latin America than to Spain. In the United States, the term was not coined by the *gringos*, but emerged from the *gente*, the people themselves."

Some prefer to use neither of the popular terms. In *Latino USA*, Ilan Stavans imagines a dialogue between two characters. One says, "'I was born in Puebla, Mexico. I was told I was a *Poblano*, or a *Mexicano*.'" Another character replies, "'I come from Varadero, a tourist resort in Cuba. My father was a *Habanero*, from Havana. So he and I are both *Cubanos*.'"

As you can see, many descendants of immigrants living in the United States prefer to think of their identity in terms of national origin. Just as some people still think of themselves as "Irish" or "Italian" even though they are the second or third generation born in America, many Hispanics define themselves by such national terms as *Salvadoraña* (a female Salvadoran) or *Guatemalteco* (a male Guatemalan). Not long ago I walked past a young man in Los Angeles whose shirt stated defiantly: "NOT Hispanic, NOT Latino, *Yo Soy Mexicano!*" (I am Mexican).

A Long and Varied History

.S. Latinos also come from a wide variety of historical backgrounds. Shortly after Columbus reached the Western Hemisphere, colonists from Spain married (or raped) the Native people they found there. The Spanish also mingled with Africans, brought to the Caribbean in huge numbers as slaves. From these unions, a new people emerged—*La Raza Mestiza* (the mixed race). A century before the Pilgrims arrived in Plymouth, Massachusetts, Spanish colonists had already settled in the southern half of what is today the United States. Some Hispanic residents of New Mexico, California, and other states can claim the oldest European ancestry in the nation.

In 1898, the United States fought Spain for control of the Caribbean. As a result, America became a dominant influence in Cuba and Puerto Rico. After the Spanish-American War, Puerto Rico became a ***commonwealth*** of the United States. In 1932, the sugar economy collapsed, sending massive loads of Puerto Rican immigrants to New

communist: *someone who believed in the philosophy of communism, in which the state owns the means of production, and there is no class system.*

civil war: *a conflict between people of the same country.*

civil rights era: *the period when various minority groups fought for their rights under the U.S. Constitution.*

York. A few decades later, in 1961, the United States cut off all business ties with Cuba, where Fidel Castro had established his ***communist*** government friendly to Russia. As a result, middle- and upper-class Cubans migrated en masse to Florida.

In the first decades of the twentieth century, ***civil war*** caused many Mexicans to flee across the borders of California, Arizona, and Texas to escape from violence. Forty years later, another wave of migration headed for the United States. The 1980s in Mexico and Central America were known as the *década perdida*, or lost decade. The Mexican economy went into a depression, and brutal wars fueled by U.S. involvement engulfed Guatemala, El Salvador, and Nicaragua. Again, families fleeing poverty and warfare headed for *El Norte* (the North—the United States).

All these groups—longtime residents of the Southwest, Puerto Ricans, Cubans, Central Americans, and Mexicans—are each culturally distinct. They originally had no concept of being one group with a common title or cause. Only in the last part of the twentieth century, during the ***civil rights era***, did Hispanics in the United States begin to develop a sense of common identity.

The Latino Population Boom

t the beginning of the twenty-first century, Latinos have become the dominant minority group in the United States. In January 2003, the Census Bureau announced, "Hispanics have surpassed blacks as the nation's largest minority group." The same report provided the following details on the U.S. population: "Hispanics now comprise nearly 13 percent of

Latino teens

the U.S. population, which grew to 284.8 million in July 2001. Blacks make up 12.7 percent of the nation's population. Asians are the next largest minority group after blacks and Hispanics, at about 12.1 million, or 4 percent of the population. Whites remained the largest single population group, numbering about 199.3 million, nearly 70 percent of all U.S. residents." More recently, the Census Bureau reported that the Latino population in the United States nearly doubled between 1990 and 2004—from 22.4 million to almost 40 million.

The Latino population boom is most visible in large American cities. Latinos now make up almost 50 percent of the population in Los Angeles County, California. In seven of America's ten largest cities—New York, Los Angeles, Houston, San Diego, Phoenix,

15

This Latino child and his family live in a small town in upstate New York.

Dallas, and San Antonio—Latinos now outnumber African Americans. In four of those cities—Los Angeles, Houston, Dallas, and San Antonio—Latinos also outnumber non-Hispanic whites. In Chicago, Latinos are 27 percent of the population and hold the balance of power in most city elections.

Latinos are also adding to the growth of mid-sized cities throughout the United States. They are the fastest growing group in the state of Michigan. Holland, Michigan, traditionally known for its tulip festival and wooden shoe factory, is now home to a majority Latino population. In Reading, Pennsylvania, not far from Amish country, the most likely residents of its old brick rowhouses are Puerto Rican, Cuban, and Mexican families. Salt Lake City elementary schools report 40 percent of their population is Latino. If you are driving

Hey Gringo!

t took several paragraphs in this chapter to debate whether Latinos should be called Hispanics (or should I say, whether Hispanics should be called Latinos). So, what do we call non-Hispanic whites? Some books say "non-Hispanic whites," others say "Anglos," and some just say "whites." But in Mexico, Central America, or in U.S. *barrios* (Latino communities) you'll hear another term—*gringos*. The term began during the Mexican-American War when American soldiers rode into Mexico singing the popular song, "Green Grows the Lilac." This sounded like "Green Goes the Lilac." So, as a joke, the Mexicans started calling the soldiers "green goes" (*gringos*). The word has stuck until today.

through Nashville, Tennessee, the country music capital of the world, listening to radio, however, you will notice the city has a new sound—three of its music stations play only Spanish-language tunes.

Large families are the major cause of this remarkable Latino population growth. Two out of three Latino Americans are Mexicans, and Mexican-born mothers living in the United States will have on the average twice as many children as non-Hispanic mothers. The most popular name for boys born in both California and Texas in 1999 was José. According to U.S. Census Bureau predictions, Latinos will supply two-thirds of popula-

Latina students

tion growth in the United States for the first half of the twenty-first century. At this rate, Latinos will number 80 million by the year 2050. The Census Bureau estimates that the white non-Hispanic population will grow about seven percent between 2000 and 2050, while the Hispanic population will increase by 194 percent. Shortly after that, non-Hispanic whites will become a minority group, numbering less than half of the U.S. population.

Already, Latinos have made a significant impact on the broader American culture. Saucy Latin rhythms can be heard every hour on pop radio stations. Moviegoers flock to see Latinas and Latinos on the silver screen. Tacos are about to replace hamburgers as the staple of American fast food. *Cinco de Mayo* and *Dia de los Muertos* join Saint Patrick's Day on city holiday calendars. Such changes may seem superficial, but the popular tastes of the nation are an indication of greater changes to come. Every ten years, someone declares "the decade of the Latino," but the past few decades will be nothing compared to the influence Hispanics are going to have in America *mañana* (tomorrow).

Habla Español

los Estados Unidos (los ace-tah-dohs oo-nee-doce): the United States

gente (hane-tay): people

la Raza (lah rahs-ah): the race, Latinos

Slicing Up the Latino American Pie

ocial commentators have lumped together a number of different groups under the term "Latino." You can see by this chart how these various groups, shown as a round "pie" chart, divide up. (From *Hispanic Market Handbook*, page 82.)

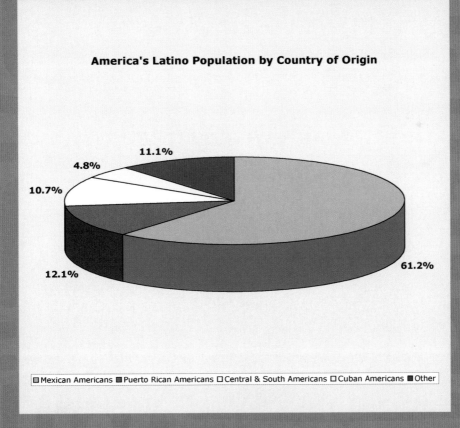

America's Latino Population by Country of Origin

11.1%

4.8%

10.7%

12.1%

61.2%

☒ Mexican Americans ■ Puerto Rican Americans ☐ Central & South Americans ☐ Cuban Americans ■ Other

2

The United States and Latin America

Old ideas die hard. Christopher Columbus dedicated his life to the idea that the Orient could be reached by sailing from Europe due west across the Atlantic Ocean. For years, he tried to pester the Portuguese Crown into giving him a ship for the voyage. They assembled a team of scientists who debated his ideas and dismissed them.

In the fifteenth century, Europeans were unaware of what lay beyond their own hemisphere.

Contrary to what you may have heard, no one then believed the world was flat. They knew it was round. The question wasn't whether one could sail to the Orient; the issue was how far and how long the journey would be. Columbus had miscalculated the size of the globe. He assumed the world was less than half its actual size. Scientists correctly stated that he would run out of supplies and starve before his ship made it halfway to the Orient. They had no idea that the entire Western Hemisphere lay undiscovered in the midst of that ocean.

Columbus took his ideas to Spain. There, this crazy but determined man eventually persuaded the monarchs Ferdinand and Isabella to gamble three ships. On October 12 of 1492, a date celebrated annually in Latin America as *Día de la Raza* (Day of the Race), Columbus's dreams were rewarded when a lookout on the *Pinta* shouted, "*Tierra! Tierra!*" (Land!)

cartographer: someone who makes maps.

To the day he died, Columbus was convinced he had reached the Orient. He and his sailors kept hoping that the palace of the Great Khan, along with the jewels and gold of the East, were on the next island ahead of them. As other navigators mapped out the contours of this new continent, it dawned on them that this was, as they called it, the New World. The honor of naming this vast continent went to Amerigo Vespucci, who convinced the **cartographer** Martin Waldseemuller to place Amerigo's name on his map of the New World.

Of course, the "New World" was hardly new to the millions of people who had settled the Western Hemisphere more than 10,000 years before. Hundreds of distinct American Indian cultures covered the Americas. The largest cities in the New World, the Inca capital city of Cuzco, Peru, and the Mexica capital Tenochtitlan (modern-day Mexico City) were as large, cleaner, and more efficiently administrated than any city in Europe at the time.

But as we said, old ideas die hard. Columbus wasn't able to accept the reality of the world he had found. Likewise, many people living in the United States today continue to remain ignorant of the realities of the Western Hemisphere. We especially tend to ignore the importance of Latin America and its continuing influence on the United States.

Choosing Your Words

irst off, the United States is *not* the same as "America." At least, not in the minds of millions of Latin Americans. A dictionary entry explains, "The Americas (sometimes referred to as America) is the area including the landmass located between the Pacific Ocean and the Atlantic Ocean. The term also includes the islands in and around the Caribbean Sea." While citizens of the United States tend to talk about "North and South America" as if they are two separate continents, most Spanish-speakers regard the entire landmass as one continent, "America." They sometimes question why people in the United States call just their country "America"—as if they owned the whole continent. In the United States, most folks use the term "American" to refer to a citizen of that country. The Spanish language, however, uses *norteamericano* (North American) or *estadounidense* (literally "United Statesian") when referring to U.S. citizens.

Some Basic Geography

atin America refers to the Spanish-speaking nations from Mexico south to the tip of South America, covering more than 8 million square miles (20,719,900 square kilometers). The United States' closest Latin American neighbor, regarded as part of North America along with Canada and the United States, is Mexico, more than 700,000 square miles (1,812,990 square kilometers) in size and home to more than 101 million people.

Beneath North America is a narrow section of land called Central America, or Mesoamerica. The countries here are said to experience "eternal spring," as they are located just above the equator.

Below Mesoamerica, we come to South America, covering 6,878,000 square miles

(17,813,900 square kilometers). As you travel below the equator, seasons become the opposite of what they are to the north. When it is summertime in northern Canada, it is winter down in Argentina.

The Caribbean Islands are also part of the Western Hemisphere. Caribbean nations include Puerto Rico, Cuba, the Dominican Republic, and Haiti. Haiti and the Dominican Republic both share the Island of Hispaniola, but French-speaking Haiti is not considered part of Latin America.

This map shows the extent of Spanish colonization in the Western Hemisphere.

Myth Busting

nglish, the official language of the United States, tends to minimize the importance of Latin America. Likewise, historical myths cover up the importance of Hispanic contributions to the United States. The myths go something like this: "English-speaking Protestants sailed to what is now the United States, declared independence from Britain, and proceeded to bravely colonize the wilderness from sea to shining sea. Since then, darker-skinned Spanish-speaking people have been trying to get in from the south and change the country." The "American" history myth may not always be stated so bluntly, but this basic outline is often assumed.

In fact, the United States has always been shaped and influenced by Latin America. Approximately a third of what is today the United States was settled and owned first by Spain, and then by Mexico after its independence from the mother country. Many Latino citizens of the United States are descended

conquistadors: *Spanish conquerors.*

The Spanish influence is seen in the architecture across the Southwest.

from *conquistadors* and colonists who settled into these regions decades before the first English settlements began on the East Coast. Early Spanish settlers gave five major states their names: California (named by the conquistador Hernán Cortés after a place in a popular Spanish poem), Colorado (red-colored), Florida (flowery), Montana (mountain), and Nevada (snow-covered).

Spanish explorers and settlers named hundreds—perhaps thousands—of places in the United States. Boca Raton, Florida, is named after jagged rocks on the ocean shore, thought to resemble a rat's mouth. The name of Las Vegas, Nevada, refers to the grasses seen growing beside spring-fed desert streams by early Spanish explorers. Of course, Los Angeles means "the Angels," but is actually short for *Nuestra Señora Reina de Los Angeles* (Our Lady the Queen of Angels). San Antonio, Texas, is named after Saint Anthony, and San Francisco, California, after Saint Francis. The prevalence of Spanish place names in the United States should give pause to those who insist on an English-only nation.

Connections between today's Mexico and the southwestern part of the United States predate even the conquistadors. The Mexica (Aztec) people have a detailed history of their migration south into Mexico from a place they called Aztlán. Scientists are uncertain exactly where this place of origin was located; theories include California, Arizona, and Utah. The oral traditions of Zuni Pueblo in New Mexico include a group who left them and headed to "the land of eternal sunshine" in the south. Archaeology has also documented trade connections between the Mexica and other Indian groups located in what is now the United States. Some Mexicans who have migrated recently from their country to the southwestern United States have understood their move as returning to the place their ancestors started from—Aztlán.

Latino United States is the Fifth-Largest Latin American Nation—and Soon to Be the Third

The significance of Latino presence in the United States can be seen by considering the answer to this question: If U.S. Latinos were counted as a separate Latin American nation, how would their numbers compare with the rest of Latin America?

At present they would be the fifth-largest Latino nation, behind Brazil, Mexico, Colombia, and Argentina. By 2050, they would be the third-largest Latin American nation.

An Important Language

The Spanish language has a long and important history in the lands now known as the United States. Basque sailors first brought Spanish to Newfoundland before 1500. In 1565, the Spaniards founded St. Augustine, Florida, the oldest continuously occupied European city in the territory of the United States. The first reading grammar text in the United States was written in Spanish in Georgia in 1658.

The Río What?

he Río Grande River is considered the border between Latin America and the United States. It runs along the national borders of Texas. Anglos call it the Río Grande, but Mexicans refer to it as Río Bravo. This river has been called many names throughout its history: Río Caudaloso, Río de Buenaventura del Norte, Río de Concepción, and Río de las Palmas. It has played an important role in history for more than four hundred years; it is now in ecological crisis from pollution and shortage of water.

Latino History 101

ar between the United States and Mexico ended in 1848 with the Treaty of Guadalupe Hidalgo. The defeated Mexican government granted to the United States parts of the modern-day states of Texas, Colorado, Arizona, New Mexico, and Wyoming, and the whole of California, Nevada, and Utah. The treaty did not specify language issues, but guaranteed the Mexican residents of these states would "be free to continue where they reside" without hardships imposed on them.

California's first *constitution* included a guarantee of Spanish-language rights: "All laws, decrees, regulations, and provisions emanating from any of the three supreme powers of this State, which from their nature require publication, shall be published in English and Spanish." Both English and Spanish are official languages in New Mexico, and Spanish has been spoken around northern New Mexico, southern Colorado, and the Mexican border since the seventeenth century.

In a sense, Latinos in the twenty-first century are merely reestablishing the importance of their presence in the United States. They have always been here, playing a vital role, but have not received due recognition. It is time to wake up and smell the coffee (probably grown in Colombia, Mexico, or Guatemala). In the coming decades, Norteamericanos will have to be better informed and more appreciative of the connections between los Estados Unidos and Latin America.

constitution: the written rules and principles governing a country.

Visitors to Santa Fe enjoy the mixture of Latino and Native crafts for sale.

⊞abla ⊞spañol

grande (grahn-day): big

río (ree-oh): river

café (cah-fay): coffee

3

The History of the Race

César Chávez, the child of *migrant farm-workers*, was born to a life of hard work. His parents loved their children and did all they could for them, but their lives were not easy. Migrant workers had to be constantly on the move in order to get jobs that changed with the farm seasons. They had no permanent homes but lived in tiny dirty cottages, which often lacked electricity or running water. It was hard for migrant children to get a good education. When he was growing up, César attended more than thirty different schools.

migrant farmworkers: agricultural workers who travel from place to place.

31

César Chávez

After graduation, César went to work full time in the fields. He was frustrated by the ways farm owners mistreated the workers, breaking promises, not paying enough, and not providing safe and decent work conditions. In 1962, Chávez decided to devote himself to the full-time task of organizing the workers into *unions*. He drove every day to different workers' camps, urging them to join. Meanwhile, César's wife had to work in the fields to feed their children. After six months, César gathered three hundred members of the new Farm Workers Union in Fresno, California. It was the beginning of *La Causa* (the Cause).

La Causa

rom their start, the United Farm Workers were committed to nonviolence as a means of bringing about justice. Although workers who joined the union were beaten, unfairly fired, and otherwise mistreated, Chávez insisted that they would only use peaceful strategies.

Several times, Chávez went on prolonged fasts—refusing to eat for weeks for the sake of justice. After one of these fasts, he told a reporter: "Our struggle is not easy. Those who oppose us are rich and powerful and they have many allies in high places. We are poor. Our allies are few. But we have something the rich do not own. We have our bodies and spirits and the justice of our cause as our weapons. I am convinced that the truest act of courage, the strongest act of manliness, is to sacrifice ourselves for others in a totally nonviolent struggle for justice."

In 1970, Chávez led the United Farm Workers Union in a strike for fair wages from California growers. Seventeen million Americans boycotted grapes as a show of support for the union. In July of 1970, twenty-six major California grape growers signed contracts with the United Farm Workers Union. They promised protections and higher wages to growers. Chávez and his nonviolent strategies for change had brought them victory.

César Chávez died in his sleep on April 23, 1993. He was in Yuma, Arizona, helping that state's farmworkers in their struggle for justice. Chávez was committed to La Causa to the very end. On August 8, 1994, President Bill Clinton **posthumously** awarded the Presidential Medal of Freedom to César Chávez. He was the first Mexican American to receive this honor.

unions: organizations that represent the workers.

posthumously: after death.

33

Castillo de San Marcos, an ancient Spanish fort in Saint Augustine, Florida

A Long, Sad Story

ésar Chávez's struggle for justice is just one chapter in the long and sometimes tragic history of Latinos in the United States. The story begins with Ponce de Leon, who arrived in Florida in 1513. Not long after that, another expedition, this one led by Pánfilo de Narváez, trekked through Florida, Louisiana, and Texas.

The Narváez expedition was a disaster. All but a handful of men died. One survivor, Cabeza de Vaca, wrote about his adventures living among the Indians from 1528 to 1536. His book *The Journey and Ordeal of Cabeza de Vaca* might remind modern readers of the movie *Dances with Wolves*—except de Vaca's story is true! Adopted by Texas Indians, Cabeza de Vaca was cast in the role of medicine man. He and several companions walked some 2,500 miles, from Texas's east coast to Mexico City. As a result of his experiences, Cabeza de Vaca was the first European to learn how Native Americans thought and felt.

Another conquistador, Hernando de Soto, led six hundred men through the southeastern United States from 1538 through 1542. His company marched through lands that today are covered by eleven different states. De Soto was frustrated in his attempts to find gold, and instead he enslaved, raped, and fought against a number of Indian tribes. De Soto's men left a bitter reminder of their visit: they introduced diseases that wiped out entire Indian nations.

At about the same time, Francisco Vasquez de Coronado led another set of explorers through the Great Plains and southwestern deserts of the United States. Coronado was driven by tales of the Seven Cities of Cibola, legendary towns filled with gold. The Indian pueblos of Zuni and Acoma, whose adobe walls sometimes appear golden when viewed from a distance, may have inspired these rumors. Like de Soto, Coronado attacked a number of peaceful Indian villages and took slaves, but ultimately, he returned penniless.

In 1565, Spanish conquistadors established the colony of Saint Augustine, Florida. The Spanish fortifications and buildings can still be seen there. Then in 1610, Juan de Onate brought a large number of soldiers and settlers to establish a colony in New Mexico. This was the beginning of a new phase of history in North America—permanent settlement.

Spanish colonies mistreated and exploited Native people. Workers on the *haciendas* (ranches) were treated as slaves. From the time of their arrival, the Spanish had sexual relations with the people they conquered. Indian women were often raped, part of what one American Indian author describes as "the sexual conquest of America."

Over time, however, Spaniards and Indians recognized their mutual interests. Common desires for family and home led Españoles (Spanish) and Indios (Indians) to marry. Over time, the descendants of these two peoples came to see themselves as a new kind of people: La Raza Mestiza (the Mixed Race).

In the eighteenth century, the Catholic Church established a chain of missions in what is today the State of California. Father Junipero Serra, a Franciscan priest, led this work. Although troubled by physical illnesses, Father Serra worked tirelessly.

35

Between 1769 and 1823, he established twenty-one missions in a network stretching from San Diego to San Francisco. Modern-day California was largely shaped by his efforts.

America's Destiny?

n the early 1800s, Anglo-Americans who had settled on the eastern coasts began to think in terms of "Manifest Destiny." This was the belief that God had specially chosen people of English origin to conquer and rule the entirety of North America. In 1819, the United States took Florida from Spain by force, while Anglos poured into the western part of the country.

President Andrew Jackson was deeply prejudiced against American Indians, African Americans, and Mexicans. He sought a way to wrest Texas from Mexico. When Mexico announced it would free all slaves in Texas, the Anglos living in that state demanded a revolution. At the time, the dictator Antonio López de Santa Anna ruled Mexico. He was one of Mexico's most controlling leaders. He had canceled the nation's constitution in 1824, assuming complete control of the country. Many Mexicans living in Texas were dissatisfied with Santa Anna's rule and joined with the Anglos in the fight against the dictator.

Texas did not officially become part of the United States until 1844. At the time, James Polk was President of the United States. Polk wanted not only Texas but also New Mexico and California to become part of the United States. In 1846, President Polk sent American troops to Matamoros, Mexico. The Mexicans resisted this *incursion*, and President Polk then declared war on Mexico.

Santa Anna with his advisors

In 1847, a large force of American soldiers invaded the heartland of Mexico. They sacked Veracruz, occupied Puebla, and then marched on to attack Mexico City itself. On September 12–13, the U.S. Army fought Mexican forces at the Castle of Chapultepec. It was the decisive battle of the Mexican-American War. After fourteen brutal hours, Mexican forces had to admit defeat. At that point, six young Mexican cadets, seeing that defeat was unavoidable, threw themselves, wrapped in Mexican flags, from the ramparts of the castle. These martyrs are honored to this day as *Los Niños Heroes* (The Child Heroes).

In 1848, Santa Anna was forced to sign the Treaty of Guadalupe Hidalgo, which sold the majority of Mexico's land to the United States for a mere 15 million dollars. Texas, Colorado, Arizona, New Mexico, Wyoming, California, Nevada, and Utah were added

The explosion of the Maine *helped trigger the Spanish-American War.*

to America's land. The Mexican population of those states were guaranteed "respect" by the treaty, but unfortunately, this was not always honored. Many of these Latinos were forced to do menial jobs for Anglo settlers.

The Spanish-American War

nother milestone in the relationship between the United States and Latin America came in 1898. The Spanish-American War replaced Spanish dominance in the Caribbean with that of the United States.

Cubanos had long desired freedom from the government of Spain. Among the Cuban revolutionaries was José Martí. He was the leader of the artistic movement known as *Modernismo*, which helped revitalize the importance of Spanish literature. Cuba's bid for freedom was a hot topic of discussion among immigrant intellectuals from Cuba, Puerto Rico, and Spain who frequented New York City's cafés at the end of the nineteenth century.

Early in 1898, the United States sent the battleship *Maine* to "keep peace" in a Havana, Cuba, harbor. Bigger than a football field, gleaming with white paint, the *Maine* was a formidable sight indeed—until a sudden and mysterious explosion sent it to the harbor's bottom. The American press quickly blamed the Spanish government.

At that time, newspapers in the United States were a highly profitable business. Owners and publishers fought to outsell competing papers by publishing exciting stories. They weren't very concerned whether the stories were accurate or not. William Randolph Hearst, owner of the *New York Journal*, sent famous author Stephen Crane and artist Frederick Remington to Cuba to cover the war. Remington sent word back to Hearst, "There is no war here." Hearst reportedly replied, "You furnish pictures and I'll furnish the war." Sure enough, the *Journal* and other papers were soon flooding newsstands with sensational but largely fabricated stories: "*Spanish Cannibalism*," "*Inhuman Torture*," "*Amazon Warriors Fight for Rebels*."

The United States declared war on Spain. In the Philippines, American warships blasted the Spanish fleet. In Cuba, former cowboy and future President, Theodore Roosevelt led his troop of Rough Riders to victory. When Spain was forced to surrender its Caribbean holdings after four months of battle, one foreign ambassador said, "It's been a splendid little war."

The Spanish-American War was indeed splendid—for the United States. As a result of the war, the country gained control of the Caribbean. In 1902, English was declared Puerto Rico's second official language. At that time, sugar was in high demand, and the United States profited greatly from Puerto Rican sugar fields. In 1917, Puerto Rico was declared a commonwealth of the United States, and Puerto Ricans were granted American citizenship. For a century now, Puerto Ricans have debated and disagreed whether they wish to continue as part of the United States or seek independence.

Prejudice and Riots

n the 1940s, Mexican Americans in southern California faced some of their biggest challenges. For decades before that, the Mexican Revolution and the poverty of the 1930s had driven them northward. During World War II, half a million Latinos fought bravely for the United States. At home, however, Mexican American teens, called *Pachucos*, felt the hatred of prejudice. Pachucos, or Zoot-Suiters, dressed distinctively as a statement of pride in their heritage.

On August 2, 1942, a young man named José Díaz was found dead in the road near his home. The Los Angeles police blamed a gang of pachucos for his death. The press blazed headlines about the murder and the "hoodlums" involved. They were characterized as teen menaces, bent toward violence by their Aztec heritage. The accused boys were convicted, but they were freed when their case was appealed. This incident, known as the Sleepy Lagoon Case, raised tensions between Anglos and Latinos in Los Angeles.

In the spring of 1943, the Zoot Suit Riots broke out. (Among Latinos, they are also known as "the Sailors' Riots.") A group of sailors on shore leave claimed they were attacked by a group of pachucos. Responding to this claim, more than two hundred sailors drove into the heart of the Mexican American community in East Los Angeles. They beat up every Zoot-Suiter they could find. Though nine sailors were arrested for this riot, not one was charged with any crime.

On the following nights, the navy men, now joined by members of the army, again invaded East Los Angeles. They broke into bars and theaters, assaulting anyone in their way. The police did not arrest a single sailor or soldier. Instead, they arrested over six hundred Chicano youths, most without cause. Residents of Los Angeles cheered on the servicemen. California newspapers chose to blame the victims, applauding the servicemen for rescuing a city that was "terrorized" by Mexican "zoot suit hoodlums." The Sailors' Riots revealed the extent of prejudice against Latinos in the United States during the 1940s.

Cuba and Communism

n 1958, events on the Caribbean island of Cuba sent shockwaves to America's shores. Revolutionary Fidel Castro and a small group of armed rebels overthrew the dictator Fugencio Batista. For a long time, Cuba had been a favorite vacation spot for North Americans looking to gamble and enjoy Caribbean culture. Americans were upset when Castro adopted a clearly communist political approach, abolishing private property.

While many of Latin America's poor cheered at the beginning of Cuba's revolutionary new era, they also had causes for concern. Rival politicians, church leaders, and businesspeople were treated harshly. Thousands of Cubans were executed, many of them without trial.

On April 17, 1961, a small army of fifteen hundred Cuban *exiles* landed at the Bay of Pigs on the Cuban coast. The CIA had trained them to take Cuba back from Castro. The invasion was a massive failure. In 1962, the United States began its economic *blockade* of Cuba. The government believed this would bring the communist state to its knees within a few short years. Instead, the blockade, and the Castro regime, has lasted more than forty years.

During the turbulent years when Castro assumed power, more than one million Cubans braved the ocean to sail from Cuba to Florida. In 1960, that state began the first bilingual Spanish-English schools in the United States as a way to help Cuban exiles keep their mother tongue.

exiles: those unwillingly living out of their country, often for political reasons.

blockade: an organized action to prevent the entrance or exit of people or goods from a country.

The Movement

he 1960s were a decade of phenomenal change for all people in the United States. Dr. Martin Luther King Jr. and his nonviolent struggle for minority rights set an example for other people of color. A similar contest for equal rights among Latinos was *El Movimiento* (The Movement).

Latinos acquired a new sense of pride in their culture and heritage. The word *Chicano* gained popularity as a way of describing Mexican Americans. The word comes from Xica, a part

Dr. Martin Luther King Jr. played an influential role in the civil rights movement.

"Viva Zapata!"

 he story of Emiliano Zapata proves you can kill a man but not the things he lived for. Zapata was a Mexican Indian born in southern Mexico in the late nineteenth century. In 1910, he went to Mexico City to argue for the rights of Indians, but instead, he was abducted into the army of Presidente Porfirio Díaz. Shortly after, a revolution began against Díaz. Zapata gathered a small army of poor people from his region. For almost a decade, Zapata led his forces successfully against the *federales*. Unlike fellow revolutionary Pancho Villa, Zapata could not be paid to surrender. So, in 1919, government officials asked him to come and negotiate. When he arrived at the meeting place, he was mowed down by rifle fire in an ambush. Seventy years after his death, Indians in Chiapas, Mexico, rose up in arms to demand fair treatment from the government. The name of their movement? Zapatistas.

of the larger word *Mexica*. In more recent years, the terms Latino and Hispanic have gained favor, since they are not limited to people of Mexican origin. As described at the start of this chapter, César Chávez gained national attention for the rights of migrant workers. Luis Valdez, who would later become a famous Hollywood film director, formed a theater troupe, *El Teatro Campesino*. This theater group expressed the message of Chicano liberation through their performances. The Brown Berets in East Los Angeles and the Puerto Rican Young Lords on the East Coast organized to lead protests. Latino *social activists* of the 1960s and 1970s began a movement for equal opportunity and respect continued by their children today.

social activists: people who work on behalf of the human rights of others.

 **Habla Español**

causa (cow-sah): cause

huelga (wale-gah): strike

federales (fay-day-rah-lays): federal troops

conquistadores (con-kees-tah-doe-rays): conquerors, the name given to the Spanish knights who fought against American Indians for control of the New World

44

Larger Than Life: Icons of Latino History

When he was executed in 1967, CIA officials and even the President of the United States were elated. He was regarded as one of the most dangerous enemies of democracy.

Thirty-seven years later, he is an American pop *icon*. Fashionable T-shirts bear the image of his smiling face, looking like some present-day hipster with his goatee and beret. Surprisingly, few of the people who wear his image are actually familiar with his life and teachings. His name? Ernesto "Che" Guevara.

icon: a symbol of a cultural or spiritual concept.

45

A street mural portrays three Latino heroes: Pancho Villa, Zapata, and Che Guevara.

As Latinos in the United States gain in numbers and influence, the heroes of Latin American history gain recognition as well. Many of these are folk heroes from south of the border rather than the United States, but they have also become part of the United States' cultural history as U.S. Latinos tell and retell their stories.

Mexican American Robin Hoods

s a result of the 1848 Treaty of Guadalupe Hidalgo, thousands of Mexicans suddenly found themselves living in part of the United States. Mistreatment from their gringo neighbors caused resentment. As a result, several men emerged as folk heroes who robbed from the rich Anglos in order to give to their poor Hispanic brethren. These *banditos* were reviled, hated, and feared by the wealthier *rancheros*, but they were applauded by the poor laborers of their time. They are still honored by songs and stories in the Southwest.

Joaquin Murrieta was one of the most famous bandito heroes, although it is difficult to know how much of his life is myth and how much is history. According to tradition, he was a Mexican miner working in California around 1850. Some say Anglos raped his wife; others say he was beaten by a gringo gang. In any case, Murrieta gathered a group of *pistoleros* to his cause, and they fought injustice until he was captured and beheaded by Texas Rangers.

A similar hero was Gregorio Cortez. He was falsely accused of stealing a horse, and he shot a sheriff in self-defense. Afterward, he eluded the authorities for some time, despite a large reward offered for his capture. He was eventually arrested, but President Lincoln pardoned him. After his release, enemies poisoned him.

Tiburcio Vasquez was another Mexican American who took the law into his own hands when the U.S. government failed to protect his people from aggression. He once said, "I believe we were unjustly deprived of the social rights that belong to us. Given $60,000 I would be able to recruit enough men and weapons to revolutionize Southern California." In 1873, Vasquez and his men robbed a hotel in Kingston, Arizona. The townspeople heard of the robbery, gathered together, and shot it out with Vasquez. He and his men escaped, but as a result of this and other escapades, a posse was organized to pursue the bandit. In March of 1874, Vasquez was hanged.

José Martí

 ot many people are respected by both the supporters of Castro in Cuba and Cuban exiles in Miami. José Martí is one of those few. He was both a man of letters and a man of action. Though he was born and died in Cuba, he spent most of his life in

José Martí

exile. He spent many years in New York, and became part of the literary and political story of Hispanic influence in the United States. Martí was born in Havana in 1853. At age sixteen he was arrested as an *Indipendista*, a supporter of Cuba's independence from Spain. He was banished from his island home.

As an exile, he lived and traveled in Spain, Mexico, the Dominican Republic, and the United States. He worked as a journalist and influenced people in Florida and New York to support the Cuban Revolutionary Party. As a poet, he was one of the founders of the Modernismo literary style. Modernismo writers express themselves in sights and sounds, rather than mere statement.

José Martí felt he could not urge others to fight a war if he was not willing to risk his own life. In 1895, he returned to his homeland with a small crew of fighters. Though he hardly knew how to shoot a gun, he threw himself fearlessly into the revolution. He died in a cavalry charge. Taking a bullet in the chest, he fell backward off his steed and lay staring at the sun. Curiously, years before that day, he had described in a poem his desire to die facing the sun.

A street mural of Pancho Villa

Francisco "Pancho" Villa

bandoleers: soldiers' belts with loops or pockets for storing ammunition.

 e rides recklessly on his mustang, swaying in the saddle to evade enemy bullets. *Bandoleers* filled with ammunition cross his chest, and a broad-brimmed Mexican hat crowns his head. With one hand he guides his steed; in the other, an ivory-handled Colt .45 spews hot lead into the cowering ranks of the opposing federales. Few men present an image so wild, romantic, and fascinating as Pancho Villa.

Villa is hero to a wide variety of people. His image can be seen on a Chicago street mural, in a Michigan restaurant, and on posters for sale on Los Angeles's Olvera Street. Mexican to

machismo: *extreme manliness, which may include such traits as courage and physical strength.*

rustling: *stealing livestock.*

mercenaries: *those who fight for money rather than political beliefs.*

the core, he also became a legend, even during his lifetime, in the United States. He was a Wild West cowboy and radical revolutionary who was utterly **machismo**. Yet feminists can be encouraged that he fought alongside *soldaderas* (female soldiers).

In 1976, his body was reburied in the Monument to the Mexican Revolution, in Mexico City (minus the head, which was stolen long ago). This honor was further proof of Villa's esteem among Mexicans. All this adoration is rather surprising, considering that the man behind the legend could be brutal.

He was born in Durango in 1877, with the name Doroteo Arango. At age sixteen, he fled from the ranch where his family lived after he shot the ranch owner's son, supposedly for raping his sister. To evade the law, he changed his name to Francisco Villa and fled to the Sierra Mountains, where he gathered a group of men around him. They lived by **rustling** and robbery. Villa and his men joined Francisco Madero's revolutionary forces in 1910. Over time, Villa recruited an army of thousands, including **mercenaries** from the United States.

Villa became something of a folk hero in the United States. Hollywood filmmakers traveled to Mexico to record his battle exploits, including some staged solely for the benefit of the Hollywood crews. A film titled *And Starring Pancho Villa*, based on Villa's relationship with moviemakers, was recently released. Antonio Banderas plays Villa, and it gives an informative yet entertaining picture of Pancho's life.

Villa's forces were based in the State of Chihuahua. There, he ruled like a dictator. He supported his army by stealing cattle herds in Mexico and exchanging them for guns and ammunition north of the border. He issued his own money. If anyone refused to take it, they ran the risk of being shot.

Villa was truly a champion of the poor, redistributing the property and money of wealthy landowners among his ragtag army of followers. At the same time, he could be merciless. He ordered people to be killed by firing squads, often on a whim. Officers who failed their assignments risked execution. He married twenty-six times, ending previous marriages simply by raiding towns and destroying the marriage records!

When the United States got involved in Mexico's revolutionary war—on the side of the government—Villa fought back. He raided the border town of Columbus, New Mexico, killing U.S. civilians. Americans saw Villa as a terrorist, while the poor in Mexico saw him avenging decades of oppression by the gringos. General Pershing and the U.S. Army spent months chasing Villa, but even with airplanes and armored cars, they were unable to catch him.

Villa could not be defeated, but he could be bribed. The government paid him to retire from fighting. He settled down on a large ranch, where he enjoyed cockfights and women. In 1923, he was ambushed and killed while returning from a business trip. In death, he became even more famous than in life. As one biographer said, "He was hated by thousands yet loved by millions."

Ruben Salazar:
A Modern-Day Martyr

any people sacrificed in one way or another for the Chicano civil rights struggle of the 1960s known as El Movimiento. It cost Ruben Salazar his life.

Salazar was born in Juárez, Mexico, on March 28, 1928. His parents, Luz and Salvador Salazar, moved the family to El Paso a year later. He graduated from El Paso High School, then served two years with the U.S. Army in Germany. After serving with the armed forces, he studied at Texas Western College and earned a bachelor's degree in journalism in 1954. At his first newspaper job, he worked for the *El Paso Herald-Post*. He was well known for his bold stories about the lives of Chicanos living near the border, presenting a reality unknown to many Anglos at the time.

By the late 1960s, Salazar was an award-winning journalist for the Spanish-language television station KMEX. He also wrote a weekly editorial for the *Los Angeles Times*. He was bold and outspoken, especially regarding police brutality with Chicanos.

On August 29, 1970, the streets of Los Angeles were filled with conflict. Thirty thousand people, from all different races, marched that day to protest the Vietnam War. The police came in to squelch the marches. Late in the afternoon, Ruben Salazar and his news crew went into a tavern called the Silver Dollar Café. For reasons that have never been fully explained, deputies from the L.A. County Sheriff's office surrounded the bar. They fired tear gas canisters through the front door. Salazar was hit in the head and died instantly.

Salazar's friend Earl Shorris wrote, "He was not the first Latino reporter or even the first Latino columnist, but he was the best and the bravest." Laguna Park, at 3864 Whittier Boulevard in East Los Angeles, was renamed Ruben Salazar Park. The park is the location where L.A. County officers brutally treated the demonstrators on the day Salazar was killed.

Ernesto "Che" Guevara

s we said at the beginning of this chapter, Che is perhaps the most famous of all Latino heroes. He is very much an icon on the streets of East Los Angeles, where the great majority of residents are Latino. His face looks down from posters on music store walls, in murals on the sides of buildings, and on T-shirts. Curiously, Che is just as popular in upstate New York, where the population consists almost entirely of Anglos. Che has become a legend, not only with Latinos but also with North American young people of all races. It is an odd twist that Che's image has become a device for selling clothes and other items. Very few of the people who idealize Guevara will ever make the kinds of sacrifices he made for his beliefs.

Ernesto Guevara was born in Rosario, Argentina, on May 14, 1928. When he was two

A Latino toddler sits beneath the family portrait of Che Guevara.

years old, Ernesto developed severe asthma that would trouble him for the rest of his life. Because of his asthma, Ernesto was unable to attend school, so his mother taught him to read and write at home. He was extremely intelligent, learning more than most children of his age.

In 1950, when he was twenty-two, Guevara was accepted into Buenos Aires University where he studied medicine. While he was in college, Ernesto traveled around the northern part of Argentina on his motorcycle. For the first time in his life, he saw that the wealthy area he grew up in was different from the rest of Argentina. Everywhere he traveled he saw poverty. As a result, Ernesto committed himself to helping poor, common people.

When Guevara graduated from the university, he headed to Guatemala, where a revolution was taking place. At the same time, he began reading about *Marxism.* In Guatemala, he supported the Arbenz regime, which was fighting against CIA-backed rebels. He signed up to fight but was asked to serve instead as a doctor. In June 1952, the Arbenz government was beaten, and Guevara fled to Mexico.

In July of 1955, Ernesto met Fidel Castro. He became interested in Fidel's plot to overthrow the corrupt Batista dictatorship and volunteered to be a doctor for the small rebel army. Even though he still suffered from asthma, Guevara excelled in the rebel boot camp.

On November 25, 1965, the rebels left Mexico on a small boat headed to Cuba.

When they arrived on the island, the rebels were attacked and defeated. Fifteen *guerrillas*, including Guevara and Castro, survived the attack, but they had only nine weapons. Amazingly, this tiny defeated group fought back, over the years gaining followers until they took control of the nation.

At this time, Ernesto became known as "Che," an Argentine expression similar to "Pal" or "Buddy." The Cuban rebels called him that as a way of showing their friendship while honoring his Argentinean origin.

Che showed remarkable courage under fire. He became second-in-command of the revolutionary forces. After the revolution, Guevara was given a high-ranking administrative position in the Castro regime, but he did not like the daily work of political office. He had to be with the common people, in the field, promoting revolution.

In 1966, Che went to Bolivia disguised as a businessman. There, he met with forces attempting a Marxist revolution. Once again, he lived in the jungles as a guerrilla fighter. A special group of the Bolivian armed forces, trained and equipped by the CIA, hunted him relentlessly.

On October 8, 1967, Guevara was wounded in action and taken prisoner. The CIA informed American President Lyndon Johnson. The next day, the Bolivian commander in the field ordered Che's execution. The soldier chosen for this task trembled when ordered to put to death such a legendary figure. Guevara looked him in the eye and said, "I know you've come to kill me. Go ahead and shoot, but know that you are killing a man."

Decades after his death, Guevara is still *controversial*. On the one hand, he can be admired for his complete dedication to his beliefs. Many communist leaders were *hypocrites*. They spoke about helping the poor while living comfortable lives. Although he suffered from asthma his entire life, Che Guevara insisted on doing every chore, carrying every load, going without food if necessary, and in every way sharing the hardships of combat with his men. He lived among the poor. He never asked others to do things he himself would not do.

At the same time, he encouraged violence. While some North American Latinos see Guevara as a larger-than-life hero, many Cuban Americans recall his legacy with anger. The Cuban revolution convinced Guevara that the poor could only win their battles if they were willing to hate their enemies and treat them ruthlessly. Guevara was responsible for killings that took place after Castro's revolution succeeded. While *radicals* may embrace him as a hero, some Cuban exiles have bitter memories of Guevara's role in the history of their country.

Marxism: the political and economic beliefs, based on Karl Marx and Friedrich Engels, that view class struggle as the driving force behind change in Western societies.

guerrillas: members of an unofficial military unit, usually operating with political motives.

controversial: causes disagreement.

hypocrites: people who claim one thing but act in a contrary way.

radicals: those who are in favor of major change.

The Mirabal Sisters

More than 300,000 immigrants from the Dominican Republic inhabit the various boroughs of New York City. Even as they become part of the cultural mosaic of the United States, they continue to venerate a brave set of sisters known as *Las Mariposas*—the butterflies. These women are especially remembered on November 25, the International Day Against Violence Against Women. On that date, in 1960, three of the Mirabal sisters gave their lives to end a brutal dictatorship.

The four Mirabal sisters, Patria, Minerva, Marita Teresa, and Bélgica, grew up at a time when the dictator Rafael Trujillo governed their nation, the Dominican Republic. In 1937, Trujillo had ordered the massacre of 20,000 Haitian immigrants. As they grew up, the sisters determined to do all they could to free their nation of this unjust leader. Patria once said, "We cannot allow our children to grow up in this corrupt and tyrannical regime, we have to fight against it, and I am willing to give up everything, including my life if necessary."

The sisters were from the upper class of Dominican society, highly educated, artistic, and influential. They organized a secret group, called Las Mariposas, to fight against Trujillo's regime. When Trujillo became aware of their work, he ordered that their husbands be arrested. The men were sent to a remote jail in the countryside, and the sisters were then invited to visit their husbands. Bélgica stayed behind to watch the children. On their way to the prison, their car was stopped. Patria, Minerva, and Marita Teresa were pulled out of the car, clubbed to death, and their bodies thrown over a cliff.

The dictator tried to explain away their death as an accident, but the truth became widely known. Rather than silence the opposition, the death of these popular and respected women fanned the flames of liberation. Political opponents assassinated Trujillo a year after their deaths. Today, the Mirabal sisters are honored in the Dominican Republic as "the Mothers of the Nation."

 **Habla Español**

machismo (mah-chees-moe): manliness

mariposa (mah-ree-poe-sah): butterfly

5

The Faith

"She is a devout, prayerful, and faith-filled woman. She adorns her *altarcito* (home altar) to the Blessed Virgin with flowers and candles. As children we knelt at the feet of the Virgin to pray the rosary together. In any family crisis Mom would remind us: *'Hay está Díos!'* (There is God)." In the book *El Cuerpo de Cristo* (*The Body of Christ*) Vicente López uses these words to describe the way his mother modeled Catholic faith for his family.

A street mural expresses the faith of Latino Pentecostals.

Latinos have characteristically been people of deep spiritual faith. In a 2001 Barna survey, researchers found that 53 percent of Latinos say the "church they attend most frequently" is Catholic. Another 25 percent identified themselves as "born-again Christian." A different survey conducted a year later by the Pew Foundation found that 70 percent of Latinos consider themselves Catholic, and 23 percent affiliate with *Pentecostal* churches. While details vary, both of these surveys point out two trends in Latino faith today. The majority of Latinos (88 percent in one survey and 93 percent in the other) identify with some form of Christian faith. A majority follows traditional Latino practice by worshiping as Catholics, though an increasing number regard themselves as "born again" or Pentecostal.

Native Spirituality

hen Christopher Columbus arrived in the Caribbean Islands, he described the natives as "*un gente que vive en Díos*" (a people who live in God). The American Indians were certainly spiritual minded, though their beliefs differed greatly from that of Europeans. From first contact, the Spanish tried to convert Native Americans to Christianity. At the same time, the Spanish slaughtered the Indians, ran them off their lands, exposed them to diseases that killed them, forced them into slavery, and raped the women. Not surprisingly, most Indians were unwilling to consider the white man's religion. One Caribbean chief, Hatuey, told a priest he hoped to die and go to hell if that meant he would not have to meet the Christian invaders of his land in the afterlife.

Nonetheless, the Raza Mestiza of Latinos today—people descended from Indians and Spaniards—are overwhelmingly Christian. How did this come about?

In the decade after 1531, some nine million Indians became Catholic due to their belief in the Virgin of Guadalupe. At the same time, Dominican *friars* such as Bartoleme de Las Casas stood against the *oppressive* practices of the conquistadors to defend Indian rights.

In the twentieth and twenty-first centuries, Latino population growth has revolutionized the Catholic Church in the United States. Between 1960 and 2002, membership in Catholic churches grew 71 percent due to the influx of Latinos. Currently, four out of ten American Catholics are Latino. These numbers pose a challenge for spiritual leadership, since there is

Pentecostal: relating to any Christian denomination that emphasizes the Holy Spirit and interprets the Bible literally.

friars: men belonging to any of a number of Catholic religious orders.

oppressive: restrictive.

spontaneous: *un-planned; spur of the moment.*

innovative: *something new or that is done in a new way.*

apparition: *something ghostly.*

sociologists: *people who study the origin, development, and structure of a society, and the behavior of the individuals and groups in that society.*

The image of the Virgin of Guadalupe appears on billboards, storefronts, and restaurants.

only one priest for every 10,000 Catholic Latinos. Serving so many is a challenge.

Father Lorenzo Miranda serves as priest at St. Louise of France Church in La Puente, California, where the church is spiritual home for thousands of Latino families, most of them first-generation immigrants from Mexico and Central America. Father Lorenzo says, "I could work all day and stay here 'til midnight just receiving people. . . . There's a tremendous spiritual hunger now." Despite the hard work, Father Lorenzo says he loves "helping people find their spiritual path."

Latinos bring their own special traditions to the Catholic Church. Hispanic masses are livelier, more *spontaneous*, and more *innovative* than Anglo ceremonies. Guitar-playing and hand-clapping are common. Father Lorenzo says, "They make the mass like a fiesta."

All Catholics believe in the Virgin Mary and the saints. Latinos are especially devoted to the Virgin of Guadalupe. Her image can be seen everywhere in major cities, where she appears on the walls of bakeries, repair shops, and homes. She is on shirts, tattoos, bumper stickers, and flags. Wherever she is seen, Guadalupe wears a blue cape covered with stars. Her head is bowed slightly, her lips smiling, and her hands clasped together.

The Virgin of Guadalupe

 Christian peasant and Aztec Indian named Juan Diego was walking from his home to Tenochtitlan (Mexico City) in 1531 when he beheld an *apparition* of the Virgin

Mary. She was dark-skinned, like Juan's people, and she addressed him in *Nahuatl*, the Aztec language. She said she was "the Mother of the One Great God" and asked to be worshiped by "all the people who live together in this land."

Juan ran to Mexico City and told the bishop, who was politely dismissive of the Indian's claims. The bishop told Juan Diego he would need a miraculous sign to believe such a thing had happened. Shortly after, Juan Diego again encountered the Virgin. She told him to take off his *tilma*, a cape woven from cactus fibers, and fill it with flowers. He did so—and when he returned again to the bishop's house and shook out the flowers, on his cape they beheld an image of the Virgin, just as she had appeared to Juan Diego.

According to tradition, Mary told Juan Diego her name was *Coatlaxopeuh*, which in the Mexica tongue means "one who treads the serpent." To Spaniards hearing the word it sounded like *Guadalupe*, a famous shrine to the Virgin in Spain. This appearance to Juan Diego became known as Our Lady the Virgin of Guadalupe.

According to Catholic believers, Juan Diego's tilma is the one seen today by tens of thousands of pilgrims who visit the Shrine to the Virgin of Guadalupe in Mexico City. The Catholic Church has declared her Patroness (protecting Saint) for all the Americas. Almost every household in Mexico, and many more in Central and South America and the United States, has an account of some answer to prayer granted by the Virgin. Mexicans are often called *Guadalupanos*.

Even when Latinos change religions, they may keep their devotion to the Virgin de Guadalupe. For example, Carlos Monsiváis offers this prayer to Guadalupe: "*Jefecita*, [lady boss] I am still faithful to you, who represents the nation, even though I now may be [Pentecostal, Jehovah's Witness, Adventist, Baptist or Mormon]." The famous Latina author Sandra Cisneros is a Buddhist by conviction, but she still talks regularly to *Nuestra Señora*. She calls herself a *Buddhalupano*.

Besides the Virgin of Guadalupe, Latino Catholics believe in many other saints. Some are official saints of the Catholic Church and others are not. One example is Toribio Romo, a priest killed in the Mexican revolution. According to many stories, Mexicans who have prayed for help crossing the border into El Norte receive help from a mysterious stranger—Saint Romo. Latino spirituality is filled with such beliefs, which *sociologists* call "folk religion," beliefs formed by the experiences of common people rather than the official teachings of the church.

Pentecostal Latinos

century ago, practically all Hispanics throughout the Americas were Catholic. Today, approximately one out of four are Pentecostals. For the most part, those attending such churches prefer to call themselves simply *Cristiano* (Christian).

The word Pentecostal comes from the second chapter of the Book of Acts, in the Christian New Testament. In that passage "tongues of fire" came upon the early Christians, "and they began to speak other languages as the Spirit enabled them." Modern-day Pentecostal churches began with the Azusa Street Mission in Los Angeles, California, in 1906, when, according to popular tradition, white, African American, and Mexican American Christians spoke in tongues and witnessed miracles of healing. The Assemblies of God Churches (*Asambleas de Dios*) and the Apostolic Churches, two large groups, sprang from the Azusa Street experience.

Faith in Action

onny Arguinzoni was a heroin addict living in southern California in the 1960s. He met Nicky Cruz, a Puerto Rican who had walked away from a gang after a Pentecostal conversion experience. Cruz told Arguinzoni, "God can free you from addiction." Sonny remembers what happened next: "Suddenly I was singing and shouting and it wasn't in English, it was in some strange language that kept flowing off my tongue." Sonny had received what Pentecostals call the Baptism of the Holy Spirit, and with it came freedom from his addiction.

Sonny Arguinzoni bought a home in Los Angeles and invited gang members and drug addicts to come and experience healing like he had. From this humble beginning, Sonny's

Old Troubles Pursue New Lives

ragedy struck twice at Homeboy Industries, between the time when the author conducted interviews and the time of this book's publication. Miguel Gomez, 34, and Arturo Casas, 25, were shot and killed in two separate incidents. They were both murdered while working to remove spray-painted gang graffiti, working for Homeboy Industries' graffiti removal program. Father Greg Boyle said whatever the reason for their shooting deaths, he knows Gomez and Casas were trying to turn their lives around. "Arturo Casas was a man who really chose to be different and to redirect his life, and that decision was genuine," Boyle said. Sadly, the violence of gang life may continue to follow former members, even after they have left that life behind. Lucky Severson, covering the story for *Religion & Ethics Newsweekly*, notes: "Arturo was the 129th gang banger Father Boyle has buried. For the time being, Father G has suspended graffiti removal. But he hasn't suspended hope."

Templo Calvario

ministry, called Victory Outreach, has grown to more than 200,000 members in more than five hundred churches.

All Latino churches, whether they are Catholic or Protestant, tend to focus on meeting the practical needs of needy people in their community. For example, Jobs for a Future is located in the Boyle Heights area of Los Angeles, where many youths are involved with gangs. This agency serves more than a thousand young people who walk through its doors every month seeking to change his or her life in a more positive direction. The workers help kids to find jobs, provide family and personal counseling, and even offer a tattoo removal clinic. They also run their own set of businesses called Homeboy Industries. Their motto is, "Nothing stops a bullet like a job."

The vision of Jobs for a Future came from Father Greg Boyle. Though not of Hispanic racial heritage, his religious beliefs were influenced by priests he encountered in Latin

Latino Spirituality from Non-European Traditions

ot all Latinos worship in Christian traditions. Some 800,000 Cubans, Puerto Ricans, and Dominicans practice *Santeria*. Former slaves brought this religion from the Yoruba tribe in Africa.

Thousands of Latinos have also converted to Islam. Many people living in the Iberian Peninsula were Muslim before "the Christian Monarchs" of Spain, Ferdinand and Isabella, crushed such beliefs with the tortures of the Inquisition. For some Latinos, Islam is a rediscovery of long-lost roots.

Traditional Native American beliefs also appeal to Latinos. Some very ancient practices are still followed by *Curanderas*, or traditional healers in Latino communities. Carlos Castaneda influenced many Latinos with his book *The Teachings of Don Juan*. It tells of his experiences with a Mexican Yaqui Indian shaman.

America. In turn, his influence has helped transform the East Los Angeles barrio. He asked himself, "*Que haria Jesús?*" (What would Jesus do?) and decided the most important thing was to love these kids whom everyone else seemed to hate. As one former gang member says, "Father G is like God, because he will never stop believing in you."

Templo Calvario (Calvary Temple), the largest multicultural Pentecostal church in the United States, ministers largely to Latinos in a Santa Ana, California, neighborhood. First, church members opened *Obras de Amor* food warehouse. Businesses donated groceries, and the church was soon feeding hundreds of needy families every week. That, however, was not enough in the church's estimation, since there were thousands more whose needs went unmet. The church organized a network of churches called Kingdom Coalition, which now has more than sixty member organizations. Kingdom Coalition provides more than 80,000 people every month with food, educational help, addiction recovery services, and other forms of aid.

Latino ministries like *Obras de Amor*, Victory Outreach, and Homeboy Industries demonstrate Virgilio Elizondo's words in his book *El Cuerpo de Cristo*:

> The first priority of the church must always be the needs of the poor, the immigrant, the abandoned, the unwanted and those in special need. This is the first priority of the Gospel and it must be ours today. We must not only minister to the needs of the poor but recognize how the poor minister to the rest of the church.

Habla Español

barrio (bahr-ree-oh): neighborhood; usually an expression for the Latino neighborhood in a town

iglesia (ee-glace-ee-ah): church

milagro (mee-lah-grow): miracle

santo (sahn-toe): saint

Milagros

Do you believe in miracles? Whether they are Catholic or Pentecostal, most Latino Christians do. For example, people come from hundreds of miles to leave small wooden crosses twined in the fence around the church in Chimayo, New Mexico—and each cross attests to an individual's faith in God's power to perform a miracle in his or her life. Chimayo is sometimes called the "Lourdes of the Southwest" because of the miracles of healing that have taken place there.

Likewise, Pentecostals stress that the Holy Spirit performs miracles today just like in the New Testament. Carmen Cannas, a member of *Iglesia Evangélica Bethel* (Bethel Evangelical Church) in North Hollywood, California, believes God healed her lungs of cancer. Carmen says, "We expect God to meet our needs. When we come to church, we expect to experience something. People come with problems—finances are short, kids are sick, and so on—and we always find an answer from God."

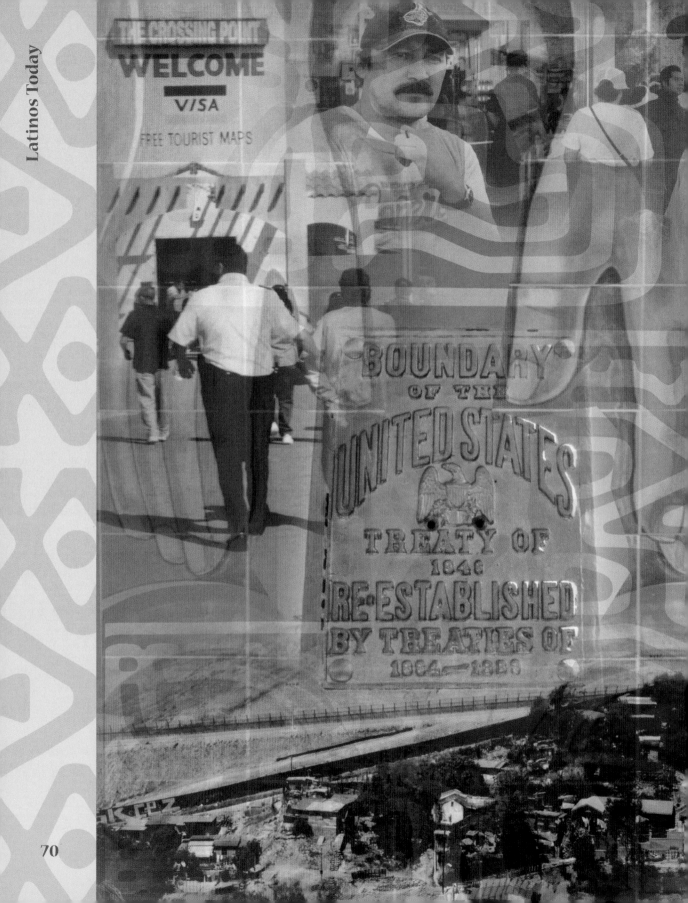

THE CROSSING POINT
WELCOME
VISA

FREE TOURIST MAPS

BOUNDARY
OF THE
UNITED STATES
TREATY OF
1846
RE-ESTABLISHED
BY TREATIES OF
1884–1886

Immigration

"Let me tell you a story about Lou Sobh, who is with us today. In 1960, he left Mexico, no money, and he couldn't speak the language. He came to America. He didn't—he couldn't speak the language at all, so he worked, and he taught himself English. He ended up becoming a janitor in a department store, a hard worker. He had a dream, and he was working toward his dream. He served in the United States Army. He got out of the army, and he had a dream to open up his own car dealership. Today, he owns fourteen—not one car dealership, but fourteen car dealerships. He employs 800 people. He's got three car franchises in Mexico. He's living proof of the American Dream.

Tijuana's slums crowd up against the U.S.-Mexican border.

"It's an incredibly important part of our nation, the Latino spirit of hard work and drive and enterprise. And, Lou, I want to congratulate you for being a success and setting an example. Thank you for coming, sir."

The American Dream

n October of 2003, U.S. President George W. Bush gave this speech. He highlighted Lou Sobh's success story in a special address, delivered in the East Room of the White House, celebrating Hispanic Heritage month. He could have picked thousands of others whose stories would also serve as examples of the "American dream."

However, Wilma Rebieiro Machado will not be among those. Wilma's route to the

American dream led her across the blistering desert of southern Arizona. She was found dead about five miles west of Douglas, Arizona, in July of 2004. When her body was found, she carried a Brazilian passport and Mexican visa. She wore light-colored pants, two shirts, and black slip-on shoes, and she carried a bag filled with prescription medications. The one thing she lacked was water.

Unfortunately, Wilma Machado is not the only person to die attempting to gain entrance into the United States. At least 1,450 people died crossing the Mexico-U.S. border between 1996 and 2000. In 2003, 205 died trying to cross the border between the Mexico and Arizona. In 2004, more fatalities had been reported per month than the previous year. Increased security at the California border has caused more border crossers to make the dangerous journey across the desert in Arizona.

The dream of a better life in los Estados Unidos continues to draw people from Latin American countries at a faster pace than ever before. Some achieve their dreams, others struggle to find their place, and some die in the attempt.

The Facts

he U.S. Census Bureau reports that of foreign-born Latinos, 52.1 percent entered the United States between 1990 and 2002, another 25.6 percent came in the 1980s, and the remaining 22.3 percent entered before 1980; 73.3 percent of those who entered before 1970 had obtained citizenship by 2002, compared with 29.9 percent who entered in the 1980s and 7.3 percent of those entering between 1990 and 2002. In 1997, 255,000 Mexican immigrants became citizens. This was more people from a single country becoming citizens in one year than ever before in American history.

A surprising number of hate-oriented Internet sites foster prejudice against Latinos by distorting the facts of immigration. Latinos as a whole are often **stereotyped** as "illegal aliens." The term "alien" means foreign or strange—in contrast to supposedly "normal" Anglo-American. In reality, however, Spanish-speaking people were already settled in today's southern United States before the Pilgrims first brought their English presence into the country. From that perspective, Anglos should be viewed as the "aliens."

Along with large numbers of Latinos whose roots in the United States precede the American Constitution, there are also millions of Puerto Ricans who are citizens by birth. Since 1917, the U.S. Congress has ruled that those who are born in Puerto Rico automatically become citizens of the United States. As you can see, many Latinos have a heritage as U.S. citizens that is older than that of some Anglo-Americans.

In many cases, the U.S. government has welcomed and invited Hispanics to come across its borders. Since Castro seized power, 1.2 million Cuban immigrants have crossed from their island home to the United States. Because the United States has firmly opposed Castro's regime, citizens of the island arriving in this country have been favored with political refugee status and benefits.

Political refugee status is not given, however, to all persons fleeing political persecution. In the 1980s, the government of Guatemala engaged in the slaughter of Mayan Indian villages in the highlands. Fleeing death, hoping to begin life anew in a land of safety and freedom, many of these people had to cross into America illegally since the government of Rios Montt, *presidente* at that time, was supported by the United States.

Legal Immigrants

housands of Latin Americans legally enter the United States every year. They do so by obtaining a visa. This may be a nonimmigrant visa for tourists, patients seeking medical treatment, businesspeople conducting their affairs, students, or workers hired for a specific job—or it may also be an immigrant visa granting permanent stay. The U.S. State Department issues immigrant visas based on family relationships or employment.

First preference goes to children of U.S. citizens, then spouses of U.S. citizens, and then siblings of U.S. citizens.

Immigrant visas can take a long time to obtain; qualifying people from Latin American countries sometimes have to wait years. They are also expensive. In 2002, it cost $325 just to apply. That's a lot when you consider the average monthly salary in Central America that year was around $100.

Once an immigrant is here with her visa, she can remain in the country by obtaining a green card or becoming a natural-ized citizen. The green card isn't actually colored green, but it's called that. Green card holders are permanent residents and must pay taxes and are eligible to be drafted into the armed services. Two years after attaining a green card, immigrants may apply for citizenship.

stereotyped: made a judgment based on incomplete, often inaccurate information.

amnesty: a period when illegal activities can be admitted to without prosecution.

Illegal Immigrants

housands of Latin Americans also attempt to enter the United States without legal documents. Wealth and oppor-tunity draw many to El Norte. In 2002, the Pew Hispanic Center conducted a survey to discover how many undocu-mented Latinos live in the United States. They estimated there were 7.8 million, of which 4.5 million came from Mexico. (Contrary to many people's stereotypes, however, four out of five Hispanics in the United States are either citizens or have proper documentation.)

In January of 2004, President Bush announced an *amnesty* proposal for illegal residents of the United States. This has

An illegal entrant is walked back across the border.

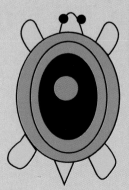

75

caused the number of illegal entries to increase dramatically. The proposal doesn't really offer amnesty, but people in Mexico have understood it that way. In fact, the President's announcement offers only the opportunity to work in the United States for three to six years before eventually applying for citizenship. As of July 2004, the plan had not gone into effect.

Illegal entry into the United States can be long, expensive, and sometimes ends in tragedy. Since September 11, 2001, security on U.S. borders has increased each year. Geographically, the border is a 2,000-mile long line of dirty river water, metal fences, barbed wire, and—where these other obstructions are missing—harsh and potentially deadly desert. Increasing numbers of officers, helicopters, robot spy planes, and electronic detection devices guard the border.

When would-be immigrants arrive at the southern edge of the border, they arrange for a *coyote*, or guide, to take them across. In 2004, coyotes below the Texas border asked between $1,500 and $2,500 American dollars per person to smuggle individuals into the United States. Usually, these funds are borrowed from a loan shark, who will later attempt to collect the money from the borrower or his family once he reaches the United States.

Choosing a coyote is an important—and possibly dangerous—decision. A good guide will safely see his "cargo" across the border, past the guards, through the barren environment, and to an American city. Sadly, many coyotes are unscrupulous or negligent. If the Border Patrol comes too near, the coyote may abandon those crossing. Or he may simply take off with the money before they arrive safely. Illegal immigrants have suffocated in unheated trucks, starved waiting in desert hideouts, and died of thirst because they were not provided with adequate supplies of water. Worse, some coyotes are bandits, who lead their charges into the desert, steal from them, and may even kill them.

Once undocumented immigrants enter the United States, they still have a hard road ahead of them. They may lack access to services, either because legal identification is re-

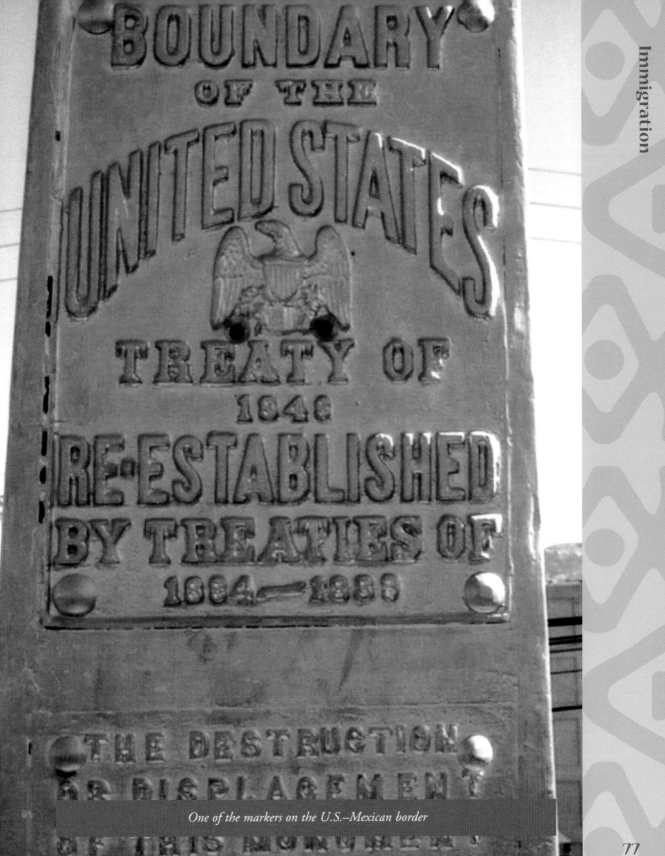

BOUNDARY
OF THE
UNITED STATES
TREATY OF
1848
RE-ESTABLISHED
BY TREATIES OF
1884 — 1889

THE DESTRUCTION
OR DISPLACEMENT
OF THIS MONUMENT
IS A MISDEMEANOR

One of the markers on the U.S.–Mexican border

quired or from their own fear of being sent back. They are likely to be stuck in low-paying jobs. At the same time, they may still make considerably more than they would in their homeland.

Sending Home More Than Love

s soon as they become established in the United States, immigrants (both legal and il-legal) from Mexico or Central America are likely to begin sending funds back to relatives in their country of origin, even if they are still living in poverty in the United States. It is estimated that, throughout the 1990s, immigrants sent more than $10 billion dollars annually to Mexico and Central America, and a number of rural communities in Latin America rely on such aid for their very existence. These so-called *migradollars* are now the largest source of foreign exchange for the Dominican Republic and El Salvador.

Hurting or Helping the United States?

n often-repeated complaint against immigrants is that they take away jobs from people already living in the United States. Such claims are not surprising, given that many Latinos arrived in the United States during a time when workers in this country lost

Money from relatives in the United States allows a family in Tijuana to install a system for running water.

their jobs. However, careful research suggests that immigration is not to blame for job loss. Studies have found that many Latino immigrants either took jobs created by the immigration itself (for example, Mexican restaurants or small clothing factories) or they took jobs that had been abandoned when people left city areas to move into the suburbs.

A U.S. Department of Labor study noted the idea that immigrants take jobs away from American workers is "the most persistent fallacy about immigration in popular thought" because it is based on the mistaken assumption that there is only a fixed number of jobs in the economy. According to a 1992 *LA Times* analysis summarizing the best available research:

> Immigrants contribute mightily to the economy, by paying billions in annual taxes, by filling low-wage jobs that keep domestic industry competitive, and by spurring investment and job-creation, revitalizing once-decaying communities. Many social scientists conclude that the newcomers, rather than drain government treasuries, contribute overall far more than they utilize in services.

Immigrants pay more than $90 billion in taxes every year and receive only $5 billion in welfare. Without their contributions to the public treasury, the economy would suffer enormous losses.

 Habla Español

migración (mee-grah-see-own): migration, leaving one's country of birth

la frontera (lah frone-tare-ah): the border

presidente (praise-ee-dane-tay): president

How to Become a U.S. Citizen

 o become a U.S. citizen, one must reside in the country for five years (three years to get a green card, then two more after that). One must also meet the following qualifications:

• be at least eighteen years old

• have no criminal record

• be able to prove five years' residency in the United States

• be able to speak English

• be able to pass a basic test of American government, history, and culture

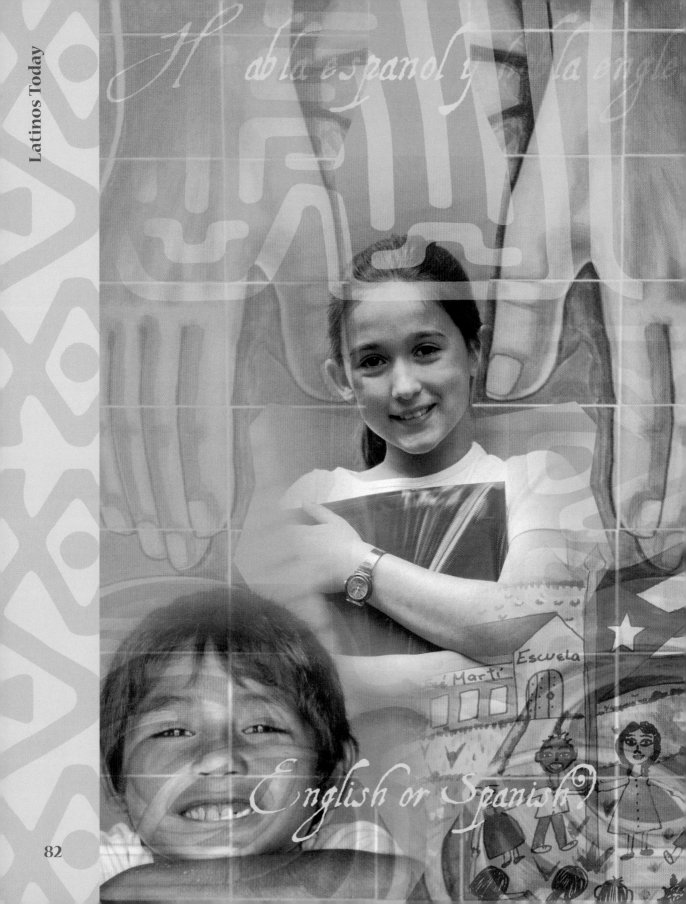

Habla español y habla engle

English or Spanish?

7

Spanish, English, or Both?

"Being bilingual gives me satisfaction and pride. When you are bilingual you can help other people, especially the needy ones. The other day I went to the pharmacy with my mom. There was an elderly couple. They did not know any English. They did not know how to explain what they needed. I helped them to fill out the prescription. At that moment I felt very proud of speaking two languages. I also feel very proud of being bilingual, because I can read, write and communicate in two languages. I feel secure to go everywhere with my parents and without them."

A Latino student takes pride in knowing both Spanish and English.

Those are the words Angel, a fourth-grade student, posted on his Massachusetts school's Web site. He is obviously very pleased with keeping his native language while also learning English.

Teresa is a student of the same age in a New York State school. Her community is predominantly Anglo, and her school offers no bilingual English-Spanish classes. She grew up with limited English in her home and has only taken courses in English. Recently, another woman tried to converse with her in Spanish. Teresa seemed a bit embarrassed and said, "I don't care much for Spanish—I like English better."

Angel and Teresa present two differing perspectives on the learning and use of language. Which is better—education in one language or two? Should Spanish-speaking students be taught in Spanish as a "bridge" to instruction in English, or should they aim to be fully fluent in both languages, taking advanced coursework in both? Which will produce more useful citizens? Which will enable students to go further in the career world? Should the United States strive to be an "English-only" nation, or give official recognition to Spanish, which is already a sort of "unofficial" second language? Questions like these continue to generate considerable heat.

Spanish-Speakers

 he 2000 Census found 11 percent of U.S. residents age five and older, or about 28 million people, spoke Spanish at home, up from eight percent in 1990, or about 17 million. While this shows there are many more Spanish-speakers in the United States, there was also indication that they continue to learn English. Among Spanish-speakers in 2000, roughly half said they spoke English "very well," about the same percentage as a decade earlier.

Although many do not realize it, the issue of Spanish-language use in the United States is centuries old. When Mexico gave up a large portion of her lands to the United States following the war of 1846–48, an estimated 75,000 Spanish-speaking people lived in the Southwest. Of these, 60,000 lived in New Mexico, 7,500 in California, 5,000 in Texas, 1,000 or so in Arizona, and 1,500 in Colorado. Not everyone agrees as to whether the Treaty of Guadalupe Hidalgo guaranteed the continued use of Spanish language in the newly acquired U.S. territories. Some argue that fair treatment of Spanish-speaking citizens would require that. English was soon used as the language of business, while Spanish remained common in households.

provision: the act of providing something.

A Cuban elementary student

When California's first constitution was drafted in 1849, the majority of the state's residents were Anglo. Nonetheless, the new constitution recognized Spanish-language rights: "All laws, decrees, regulations, and provisions emanating from any of the three supreme powers of this State, which from their nature require publication, shall be published in English and Spanish." When New Mexico became a state, its constitution also guaranteed the rights of Spanish-speakers. This included the *provision* that

> The legislature shall provide for the training of teachers in the normal schools or otherwise so that they may become proficient in both the English and Spanish languages, to qualify them to teach Spanish-speaking pupils and students in the public schools.

Bilingual Education

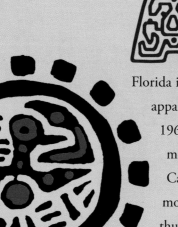

As large numbers of Cuban refugees arrived in Florida in the 1950s, the need for bilingual education became apparent. Bilingual education began in Dade County in 1960. It was designed to help the exiles retain their mother tongue. At the time, most people thought Castro's communist state would crumble within a few months, or at most a few years. Bilingual education was thus conceived of as a "short-term" strategy. However, as it became apparent that most Cuban refugees were here to stay, the understanding of bilingual education changed. It came

A Cuban school demonstrates its national pride.

Immersion may allow Spanish-speaking students to learn English from their peers.

to be seen as a way for Spanish-speaking students to gain skills in English without losing time in their general studies.

The majority of Latinos favor bilingual education. They see it as a way of keeping up the pace of education for children who have not yet learned English. They can learn math, science, and other subjects in Spanish while gaining knowledge of English. The idea is that children will gradually switch over from Spanish to English. Though immersion programs (placing a Spanish-speaking child in an all-English school environment) work well for a few children, it can cause great stress and academic failure for many others. Furthermore, many Latinos are proud of their culture and native language, and they want their children to become fully bilingual, learning English but also keeping up Spanish-language skills.

On the other hand, some Latinos oppose bilingual education. They believe it takes too long to learn English this way. There is the feeling that it segregates Latinos from other students—putting them in separate Spanish-language classes. There is also criticism that some students never learn English as well as they would in English immersion.

Not everyone agrees on the best educational approach for students like this.

English Only

ecent decades have seen fierce legal battles over the uses and limitations of Spanish language in American society. In 1980 the city of Miami, Florida, passed an "English-only" referendum. Six years later, California reversed its long bilingual tradition and added "Official English" to the state constitution. Such official English measures have now been adopted by twenty-three states. In 1996, for the first time, Congress voted and the House of Representatives approved a bill designating English as the federal government's sole language of official business.

State voters have also settled some of the most important decisions regarding bilingual education. In 1998, Californians voted for Proposition 227, "English for the Children." This bill allows for only one year of bilingual education for each child. After that,

proficiency: the ability
to do something well.

sanctions: penalizes for
breaking a rule or law.

"regardless of *proficiency*" in English, they are placed in English-only classrooms. The "English for the Children" law passed despite 63 percent of Latinos voting against it.

Dr. Juan Andrade, head of the United States Hispanic Leadership Institute, commented:

> Proposition 227 was not about "English for the Children." It was about re-institutionalizing discrimination and legalizing the deprivation of knowledge and educational opportunity. This proposition *sanctions* the rejection of Latino culture and our language in society and in the public schools.

In 2000, a similar bill, "English for the Children of Arizona," won approval due to the majority of Anglo voters in Arizona. The majority of Latinos opposed it, as did the Navajo Nation.

As the Latino population grows, and as more Hispanics become voters, public debates and votes over issues of language will no doubt continue. Some U.S. politicians and voters will continue to push for English as "the sole official language" for schools and businesses. At the same time, savvy business owners will continue to add Spanish-language labels, channels, and sales representatives, knowing how much it will increase their business.

While some shout about the need for America to be "English only," others extol the virtues of "English Plus." This movement notes the social, cultural, and educational virtues of speaking more than one language. Supporters point out that in Europe most nations require their citizens to speak several different languages. Studies show that children taught multiple languages at a young age do better in other fields as a result of their brains being stimulated. Among developed nations, the United States is unusual in encouraging its citizens to be monolingual.

Should American students be multilingual?

A young woman from Central America studies at an American college.

English, Spanish . . . or Spanglish?!

panish expressions are increasingly heard in the English language of the United States, but at the same time the English language influences the language of Spanish-speaking Latinos. It is not uncommon for Hispanics to slip "Spanglish" words into their talk. These are words that mix the two languages together. Some examples:

- *espelear*—to spell
- *lonche*—lunch
- *la marketa*—the market
- *¡Catchalo!*—Catch it!

Habla Español

maestro/maestra (mah-ae-stroe/mah-ae-strah): teacher (male/female)

alumno/alumna (ah-loom-no/ah-loom-nah): student (male/female)

aprender (ah-prane-dare): learn

enseñar (ane-sane-yar): teach

8

Business

Goya Foods is a real American business success story—Latino style. Prudencio Unanue emigrated from the Basque region of Spain to Puerto Rico in 1902, and fourteen years later he moved to New York. In the city, he was frustrated that he could not find his favorite food and cooking items such as sardines, olives, and olive oil. He also noticed that the Puerto Rican population of the city was growing, which meant it could be a strong potential market for someone starting a new business. In 1921, he married Carolina Casal, a Puerto Rican, and the same year, the newlyweds began supplying New York City *bodegas* (Hispanic grocery stores) with their favorite imported food items. By 1958, the company had its first warehouse. At that time, they focused primarily on the needs of Puerto Rican immigrants.

Goya products

In 1976, when Prudencio's son Joseph took over the company, he decided to reach the larger Latino community—not just Puerto Ricans. The company expanded its products to more than eight hundred items, including salsa, corn flour, and desserts. It continued to grow, now that they had a broader base of Latino customers.

By 1992, Goya Foods was making $500 million in profits. They decided to expand even further—outside of the Latino market. Americans were concerned about too much meat in diets, so Goya television ads suggested the healthy advantages of eating beans. They were able to expand their products into all major U.S. supermarkets.

Today, the founder's grandson, Andy Unanue, heads Goya Foods. Goya Foods Inc. is the biggest Hispanic family-owned food company in the United States. It made $750 million in sales in 2002, and it has 2,500 employees working in New Jersey, New York, Puerto Rico, Spain, the Dominican Republic, Massachusetts, Illinois, Florida, Texas, and California.

In an article for *Hispanic Trends*, Andy Unanue says stores used to be uncomfortable stocking Goya Foods products because they didn't want "them people" (Latinos) shopping there. He goes on to say,

> America has grown up enough now that the big stores do want "them people" in there. A lot has changed. Everybody loves our food, our music, there's J.Lo. . . . So if anything, the general market has accepted our product and wants to buy it, too.

The Good News

 he success of Goya Foods is just one example of the enormous effect Latino businesses and Latino consumers have on the U.S. economy. There are 1.4 million businesses in the United States owned by Latinos. Many are family businesses; more than 60 percent of these are in services or retail trade. Most common are bodegas—grocery stores that sell imported products. Also common are restaurants, clothing stores, specialty shops, repair services, and yard services. Three out of four Latino businesses are located in California, Texas, Florida, New York, and New Mexico.

Due to the rapid growth of Latino population in the United States, Hispanics have tremendous spending power. Experts tend to agree that the Latino middle class is growing. In 1998, poverty among Latinos reportedly declined by 30 percent, while average

revenues: business income.

mobility: the ability to move from one group to another.

sectors: components of an integrated system such as a society.

Latino income increased by four percent. Hispanic purchasing power was $490 billion in 2002, and Hispanic owned businesses produced over $200 billion in *revenues* in 1997.

The Bad News

t the same time, not all reports on the Latino economy are happy ones. Even as the Latino population reaches 40 million, it lags behind the rest of the country in terms of how much wealth is owned by each individual. Half of all Latinos lack a bank account. Latinos have lower home ownership rates than the rest of the population. They also exhibit dramatically lower levels of average financial worth ($10,250 compared with $99,000 for white Americans in 2000).

Mike Davis, in his book *Magical Urbanism*, notes that many recent immigrants have fallen into what he calls "*mobility* traps." That is to say, they can get certain low-paying jobs such as gardening, food preparation, house cleaning, and garment sewing, but then find it very difficult to move on to better-paying work. Despite gains for Latinos overall, he suggests that more recent immigrants actually experience "declining opportunity" economically. That is, their chances to get ahead are actually lessening now.

Two major barriers block their way to better jobs. One is poor education. Schools in areas with large Latino populations tend to be poorly funded, attract inexperienced teachers, and lack programs and resources to properly help Hispanic students. As a result, only one in twenty Latino students born outside of

The "bodega" is the traditional door for immigrants into the American economy.

the United States will graduate from college. The other limiting factor is what Davis calls "rampant job discrimination." He cites a New York study that found "racial discrimination counted for at least one-third of the current income gap" between Latino and Anglo males in the workforce. He also points out "they . . . are largely excluded from cutting-edge *sectors*" of the economy.

It is clear that many Latinos in the United States still face formidable obstacles on their way to the "American dream" of financial success.

Nonetheless, some economic forecasters continue to have high hopes for the future of Latinos financially. A Santa Barbara, California, Latino business research organization, Hispan Telligence, predicts within six years more than three million Latino companies

Richest Latinos

According to Latino Money Web site:

1. Roberto Gouizeta family
(late CEO of Coke Inc.)
$1.3 billion

2. Unanue family
(founders of Goya Foods)
$700 million

3. Tony Sanchez Jr. and family
(founder of Sanchez-O'Brien Oil)
$240 million

4. Arturo Torres
(Pizza Hut franchiser)
$190 million

5. Alex Rodrigruez
(baseball player)
$162 million

will earn nearly half a trillion dollars annually. Another report from Hispan Telligence says the buying power of Latinos in the United States has grown at nearly three times the rate of the general population. This organization predicts the number of Latino businesses and the money they earn will more than double in the first decade of the twenty-first century, and that Latino consumer spending will nearly double in that same period.

Money matters can be hard to predict. Sometimes economists disagree even on what is happening now. Latinos still face serious financial obstacles. At the same time, many are moving ahead dramatically. Whatever happens, it is clear the entire picture of business in America will be strongly influenced by Latinos in the coming decades.

Latino businesses in New York City

◫abla ◳spañol

dinero (dee-nare-oh): money

comprar (comb-prahr): to buy

vender (vane-dare): to sell

la Futura

9

The Struggle
Toward the Future

More than a decade ago, the Los Angeles
School District Junior High School was a place
where, according to one sociologist, "*dispirited*, un-
derqualified and increasingly temporary teachers are
sent as cannon-fodder into the district's massively over-
crowded and underequipped schools." The majority of
the students were first-generation immigrants from
Mexico or Central America.

*dispirited: discouraged,
a lack of enthusiasm.*

On one particular morning, the teacher had just completed roll for first period English class, when one student raised his hand. "Reina's sitting outside class crying," he told the teacher. "You better do something."

"Keep working," the teacher told the class. "I'll go talk to her."

Reina was slumped down on the walkway outside the classroom bungalow, her head in her hands. The teacher crouched down in front of her.

"Reina, what's the matter? What happened?"

She swallowed a few times; with her head down, she replied, "They shot her . . . she's dead."

"Who got shot?"

"My sister, this morning. Las Florencias [girls from the Florence gang] came to the door, they knocked . . . she opened the door and right there . . . she's dead."

The teacher didn't know what to say. "Reina . . . I'm so sorry! I can't imagine how awful you must feel."

She dabbed at her eyes, staring blankly into the fog-shrouded morning air.

"Reina . . . why are you here now? I mean, don't you want to be home with your family?"

She shook her head. "No, it's all crazy at home. The police are all over and everyone's acting crazy, and besides . . . it's not finished. Her friends are going to get even with the Florencias. Then they'll come again." The tears were starting to flow again. "I'm safe here. This is the best place I can be."

She squared her shoulders, and her voice took on new strength. "No. I'm going to go to class now. I'm going to work hard, real hard . . . every day. I'm going to get really good grades. I'm going to graduate, then go to college. I'm gonna get a job that pays good, and live where my children won't be around gangs."

rue to her determination, Reina earned mostly A's that school year. At the end of the year, she won an award for outstanding work in English. Two other teachers awarded her that year as well.

Reina is not typical of teen Latinas. Many Hispanic adolescents—probably the majority—will never be close to gang violence, or grow up in a community so beset by poverty and desperation. Today Latina and Latino teens are more likely to enjoy greater prosperity. They can focus their time and concerns on the cares common to their peers throughout the United States—dating, getting a car, and so on.

Yet there are still first-generation immigrants whose life is a struggle. A struggle to make ends meet, to avoid violence, to finish school. There are still kids like Reina who have tough choices to make. Our society must provide them with the tools they need to achieve their dreams.

Every year, the future for American Latinos looks brighter and bigger. As they become part of the American population, the values and spirit of la Raza Mestiza will enrich citizens of all ethnic groups living in the United States. And all this will be in large part due to the struggles and sacrifices of those who went before, the courageous first-generation immigrants who came to America with high hopes and determined industry.

Habla Español

antepasados (on-tay-po-sah-dohs): forefathers

lucha (loo-chah): struggle, fight

esperanza (ase-pare-on-sah): hope

105

Timeline

October 12, 1492—Día de la Raza; Columbus lands in Latin America.

1531—Near what is now Mexico City, Juan Diego sees the apparition of the Virgin Mary, Our Lady the Virgin of Guadalupe.

1565—Spaniards found St. Augustine, Florida, the oldest continuously occupied city in the United States.

1658—In Georgia, the first reading grammar book is written—in Spanish.

1848—Treaty of Guadalupe Hidalgo ends the Mexican-American War.

1898—Spanish-American War is fought over control of the Caribbean.

1917—Puerto Rico is declared a commonwealth of the United States, and its citizens are granted U.S. citizenship.

1960—Florida begins the first bilingual English-Spanish schools.

April 17, 1961—United States launches the Bay of Pigs invasion of Cuba; it is a failure.

April 8, 1993—Ellen Ochoa becomes first Latina in space.

January 2003—U.S. Census reports that Hispanics have surpassed blacks as the largest minority group in the country.

January 2004—President George W. Bush proposes an amnesty program for illegal residents of the United States.

Further Reading

Figueredo, D. H. *The Complete Idiot's Guide to Latino History and Culture.* Indianapolis: Alpha Books, 2002.

Hovius, Christopher. *Latino Migrant Workers: America's Harvesters.* Philadelphia: Mason Crest Books, 2005.

Hunter, Miranda. *Latino Americans and Immigration Laws: Crossing the Border.* Philadelphia: Mason Crest Books, 2005.

———. *The Story of Latino Civil Rights: Fighting for Justice.* Philadelphia: Mason Crest Books, 2005.

Libal, Autumn. *Cuban Americans: Exiles from an Island Home*. Philadelphia: Mason Crest Books, 2005.

Makosz, Rory. *Latino Arts and Their Influence on the United States: Songs, Dreams, and Dances*. Philadelphia: Mason Crest Books, 2005.

McIntosh, Kenneth. *First Encounters Between Spain and the Americas: Two Worlds Meet*. Philadelphia: Mason Crest Books, 2005.

———. *The Latino Religious Experience: People of Faith and Vision*. Philadelphia: Mason Crest Books, 2005.

Mintzer, Rich. *Latino Americans in Sports, Film, Music, and Government: Trailblazers*. Philadelphia: Mason Crest Books, 2005.

Sanna, Ellyn. *Latino Folklore and Culture: Stories of Family, Traditions of Pride*. Philadelphia: Mason Crest Books, 2005.

———. *Mexican Americans' Role in the United States: A History of Pride, A Future of Hope*. Philadelphia: Mason Crest Books, 2005.

———. *South America's Immigrants to the United States: The Flight from Turmoil*. Philadelphia: Mason Crest Books, 2005.

Schwartz, Eric. *Central American Immigrants to the United States: Refugees from Unrest*. Philadelphia: Mason Crest Books, 2005.

———. *Latino Economics in the United States: Job Diversity*. Philadelphia: Mason Crest Books, 2005.

Stafford, Jim. *Puerto Ricans' History and Promise: Americans Who Cannot Vote*. Philadelphia: Mason Crest Books, 2005.

Stavans, Ilan and Alcaraz, Lalo, Illustrator. *Latino USA: A Cartoon History*. New York: Basic Books, 2000.

For More Information

Hispanic Online
www.hispaniconline.com

Los Latinos USA: A Celebration of Latino Pride
www.spanishclassonline.com/usa.htm

Urban Dictionary
www.urbandictionary.com

Urban Latino TV
www.urbanlatino.com

U.S. Census Bureau Public Information Office
www.census.gov

Publisher's note:
The Web sites listed on this page were active at the time of publication. The publisher is not responsible for Web sites that have changed their addresses or discontinued operation since the date of publication. The publisher will review and update the Web site list upon each reprint.

Index

Picture Credits

Benjamin Stewart: pp. 12, 15, 16, 18, 25, 26, 29, 34, 59, 62, 66, 71, 72, 75, 77, 79, 83, 92, 95, 96, 101, 103

Comstock: pp. 88, 89

Corbis: pp. 21, 22

Cuban Art Space, Center for Cuban Studies: p. 87

MK Bassett-Harvey: pp. 6, 8, 20, 30, 44, 58, 70, 82, 94, 102

Eyewire: p. 91

Library of Congress: p. 31

Mel Rosehthal, Cuban Art Space, Center for Cuban Studies: p. 86

The National Archives and Records Administration: pp. 38, 41, 45

Photos.com: pp. 9, 10, 84

The Records of the Offices of the Government of Puerto Rico in the U.S., Centro de Estudios Puertorriqueños, Hunter College, CUNY, Photographer unknown: p. 99

The Ruth M. Reynolds Papers, Centro de Estudios Puertorriqueños, Hunter College, CUNY, Photographer unknown: p. 53

Biographies

Kenneth McIntosh is a freelance writer and former educator who recently moved to Flagstaff, Arizona, with his wife, nineteen-year-old son, and sixteen-year-old daughter. Ken lived for more than a decade in Huntington Park, California, where the city population is 97 percent Latino. He taught ESL (English as a second language) classes, English, and other subjects at a junior high school with almost entirely first-generation Hispanic immigrants. The McIntoshes have also been host parents for exchange students from Guatemala and Honduras.

Dr. José E. Limón is professor of Mexican-American Studies at the University of Texas at Austin where he has taught for twenty-five years. He has authored over forty articles and three books on Latino cultural studies and history. He lectures widely to academic audiences, civic groups, and K–12 educators.